RESCUED

by the Invisible Hand of God

Is divine intervention real and
relevant in the 21st-century?

Judy Rose Loughrey

Rescued by the Invisible Hand of God
by Judy Rose Loughrey

Published by Integrity1 Media
Aliso Viejo, CA
judyloughrey@gmail.com
707-483-4098

Cover art and book design by Anita Oneill

Ocean photo compliments of Tina Valk Wilson

Back cover quote taken from Chapter 14: Confrontation in the Hood

ISBN 13: 978-1983888885
ISBN 10: 1983888885

Dedication

Rod, I love how God created you enthusiastic, creative and forever faithful.

Eric, I love how God made you adventurous, passionate and insightful.

Todd, I love how God made you incredibly loving devoted and witty.

To my husband, my most devoted friend and confidant.

And most of all, to God, that I have miraculous eye-witness accounts to share.

Foreward

Through the years that I have been privileged to know Judy, I have found that the friend she is to me has so often been influenced by the friend God is to her. Many times the Lord so beautifuly streams through her. I believe you will find a new level of spiritual awareness as you read through these miraculous encounters the Lord has so profoundly given.

This book is a jewel in your hand. If you are one who is considering reading it, you will be stepping into the miraculous world of a faith believing woman. The threshold you are about to cross over into carries a new level of hope in the "more" God has for you. I believe the best part is that Judy's story is a bridge for your own life of miraculous encounters. Yes! You will have them. In these episodes her writing comes to life in a way that will awaken your own stories.

Corruption is permeating our society on so many fronts today, including some of our own neighborhoods. The tragedy is that many are in a state of surmising that Jesus does not exist or does not personally care. But things around us are not as they seem through our human perspective. He does so passionately care about you and our world he has so lovingly created. He has experienced our hell and knows firsthand our pain. Our Lord has indelibly scripted His presence into Judy's life story and He is waiting to do this and more in your life.

Many books and stories have been written about miracles in our world today but Judy's story is different. The holy spirit shows up in each account through the power of his love and grace reaching out to her to bring breakthrough in impossible circumstances.

I feel privileged that my life has been woven together with Judy's for some years now for her faith in Jesus has opened new doors to the miraculous for me. You are his most beloved creation. Our creator confirms your birthright as his own. It is your legacy born out of His great sacrifice, igniting a new reality of our magnificent God's grace and love who is ever present in times of trouble, to rescue us with his invisible hand.

Cynthia A. Cook, LCSW-C, Clinical Psychotherapist
Olney Psychiatric Counseling Center

Introduction

I don't know about you but miracles have always been somewhat of a mystery. From Jesus's first miracle at the wedding feast in Cana to the modern miracles of today.

Signs, wonders and miracles. We have all heard this Biblical phrase, but what does it practically mean and in what setting do miracles actually happen today? How might we open a new door in our own lives for the invisible hand of God to intervene in our times of distress and trouble?

I believe, as you will see demonstrated in this book through God's invisible hand rescuing me and those closest to me, that new doors for the miraculous may open for you and those dearest to your heart.

"Not by might nor by power but by my spirit," it says in Zechariah 4:6. But how is it so, in the realm of the miraculous? What opens the door for the fullness of His Spirit to enter into our greatest times of need?

I believe he is ready to answer this question for you as you prayerfully let Him lead you through these pages. His invisible hand is at your door. Might you open that door and invite Him to come in?

Contents

Prologue

The Power of His Love

One day in late August, 2015 my life-long friend gave me a call. She began by saying, "Judy, I think you should write a book. The world needs to know the tangible power of the living God, one who has profoundly visited you in various life-giving circumstances. Your experience has inspired me and I believe it will others." I thanked her and promptly put the idea on the shelf.

One month later my husband and I moved to Orange County, California. We joined a small group of couples who gather each week for fellowship and prayer. During the course of the first few weeks the facilitators asked, "would you be willing to share your life story so far?"

I found the question challenging but also intriguing. We all agreed and entered into our separate worlds of reruns and discoveries. I found this experience uncovered a most powerful loving God who is always present, willing and most able to rescue me from imminent danger by his invisible hand.

Psalms 107:13

Then they cried out to the Lord in their trouble, and he saved them from their distress. (NIV)

Chapter 1

Mission Impossible WWII -
16th Mission

In October of 1944 a 21-year-old U.S. Army Air Corps pilot named Russell Rose found himself sitting in the cockpit of a B-17 bomber, the famous "Flying Fortress" of World War II, flying missions over Germany. Russell and his crew of 10 had successfully completed 15 missions without incident. This was their 16th.

The skies were blue and their spirits were flying high. Russell was not called to fly lead command this day, but as they drew close to Berlin he could see those who were flying in the lead were catching a lot of flak bombarding them from the ground below. As Russell approached his target the flak began to explode all around them, penetrating the plane with unnerving force. One jagged piece came through the cockpit and caught six feet four Ted the copilot in the neck.

Russell, who was five feet nine, leaned over and placed his right hand in a tourniquet hold on

Ted's neck while he steadied the plane with his left. Suddenly he felt a jolt and, to his horror, saw one of his two right engines catch on fire. This extinguished all hope of remaining in formation as the plane began to rapidly lose altitude. Russell radioed his crew, giving them the option to bail out as he realized, with the steady loss of altitude, there was no possibility of making the hour-and-a-half trip back to Foggia, Italy. The crew of 10 quickly responded, "No, Rosie, we're riding this out with you!"

It was at this pivotal point that a picture flashed in Russell's mind. He saw himself as a young boy kneeling at his mother's knee in prayer. A new thought began to dawn and he said, "Heavenly Father if you see fit to save us, I will serve you!"

The plane began to maintain altitude although at the same time losing yet another engine. Between the loss of altitude and now the loss of engine two the plane shook in turbulent jolts. Russell held a tight grip on Ted's bleeding neck, his hand strained but sure, its strength sustained by the same force cradling the plane aloft.

Miles yet from home, Russell scanned the plane once more only to discover much to his horror engine number three was now ablaze. The integrity of the aircraft was no longer in question. Any skilled and experienced pilot could see the peril at hand and understand that a successful landing would require nothing short of a miracle.

And a miracle it was, for within a few minutes he began to see a faint outline of the landing strip ahead and a glimmer of hope began to stir in his heart. As the plane circled their destination, Russell flipped the switch to drop the landing gear knowing that he had just minutes to land before total combustion. Click. Nothing happened. He tried again. Click. Still nothing! Devoid of options, he had no other choice but to bring the enormous bomber in on its belly, one hand on the instruments and the other blood-stained hand still wrapped around Ted's neck. At this point, overcome by exhaustion, he felt an invisible hand carry them in safely as the plane came to a stop. The crew of ten immediately exited the plane leaving Russell in the cockpit still holding Ted's neck with the fire trucks and paramedics screaming toward them down the runway.

"I would have been dead within ten minutes had Russ not held my neck in that grip," Ted would later recount. The paramedics that arrived on the scene that day confirmed this, stating at the time that had the young pilot not secured his friend's jugular vein with such consistency and care, Ted would have succumbed to his injuries within minutes.

Russell knew that it could only be the hand of God that had carried them to safety that day. He was discovering that this God he had surrendered his life to was a personal God, a God who knew him, and wanted to be actively involved in his life.

After Russell's 53rd mission, General Eaker, whose jurisdiction was over the European division, called and asked him if he would consider becoming his personal pilot. Russell declined this prestigious offer, deciding instead that it was time to return home to his wife and new baby girl.

Russell's flight to San Francisco was the longest of his life. No one expected him home yet, least of all his wife Alice. After a year of military service abroad he faced rejoining civilian life and meeting a daughter whom he had only heard about through sporadic correspondence he had pored over by army-issued lamplight.

At last, landing in San Francisco, he approached the apartment where Alice lived with her parents and little Judy. Excitement flooded his heart as he rang the doorbell. Alice nearly fainted when she peeked through the lace-lined window and saw Russell standing at the door. It was a brand new reality, Russell said, when he walked in and saw his baby girl sitting in her highchair with an infectious smile on her face. A new phase of his life was in the making as he was now entering fatherhood.

A longing for time to process all that had impacted his life in the war zone began to stir powerfully within him. Finding a job on the wharf in San Francisco, inspecting fruits and vegetables was just right, and the healing process began. Two years flew by quickly and then one day, as he was eating lunch in his car, he suddenly heard an audible voice say, "Russ go be a minister, Russ go be a minister, Russ go be a minister!"

He said he would not have thought of it as he was a gifted athlete and had been accepted by the San Francisco Seals, a minor-league baseball team, before he was drafted into the war. In flight school he had graduated at the top of his class of 300 cadets in the physical as well as the written. He had been thinking of playing pro ball or going to medical school.

This was another supernatural connection from an invisible God. The voice was audible, and the call was real. Trying to digest what he had experienced in the car that day, Russell chose to delay, discussing it with Alice until he had soaked in it a while and thought it through. The following Sunday afternoon there was a surprise knock on their door. There stood a young college student who was selling Christian books, so he invited her in. He began asking her some questions that she didn't feel prepared to answer so she lined up Bible studies for him with her pastor. After nine months of studies, he and Alice decided to be baptized and thus became members of a local Christian church.

Not long after this, they decided to sell their home and Russell entered seminary, where he double majored in religion as well as Hebrew and Greek. He said, "I just can't take man's opinion on such an

5

important matter as our salvation. I must be able to read the original manuscripts for myself."

Being a most responsible husband and father, he took on a night job – six nights a week at the local Yountville veterans home. He also attended classes in the morning and sold Raleigh products in the afternoons. After two years of this rigorous schedule he was tired, and that's when a letter came in the mail from NACA with an invitation to become one of our nation's test pilots. They were offering $2100 a month plus full benefits. This was no small offer in 1948 and it looked mighty good. I was there and remember him filling out the forms, walking it out to the mailbox, and placing it inside.

That night, he said, he rolled and tossed with his decision. Then in the dawn of early morning light he finally asked, "Lord, can I accept this offer?" The answer came, "Russ, I've called you to make a difference in people's lives for eternity, will you stay the course?" The next morning after we finished breakfast, my father walked back out to that mailbox with me trailing close behind. I watched him take out the letter and proceed to tear it up. By the way, some of those test pilots became our first astronauts.

Around 1965, thirteen years now into his career as a minister of the gospel, he was approached by five Congressmen who asked him, "Russ, we would like you to consider running for Governor of California. You're a good thinker, you're fiscally smart, and we believe you're the man for the job." Life at this time was not easy. There were doctrinal problems that were not biblically based and not worthy of teaching. He had read the original manuscripts, and the Holy Spirit, as promised in John 16:13, had been leading him into truth. Being a man of character, he had taken his stand for truth. Persecution had begun from the higher-ups and the battle for biblical truth to prevail was on.

It was in the midst of this battle that the invitation came. The temptation once again was at the door. This invitation sounded like a great escape and adventure. Russell, desiring to remain true to his foxhole commitment, fell on his knees once again that night, asking the Lord if he could run this race. Once again, the answer came, "Russ, I've called you to make a difference in people's lives for eternity, will you stay the course?"

Russell stayed the course for 33 years of service to God and his people. In 1984 he contracted a cancer for which there was no cure. Once again, he rose with great courage to walk out his last battle. As I stood by his bedside I watched as hundreds of people contacted him through letters, phone calls and visits at his bedside. All with one message, "thank you so much Pastor Rose for taking the monkey off our back. We are now walking in peace and confidence that the doing and dying of Jesus Christ on this earth was enough to save us if we repent and receive His Gift of salvation. We are free!"

It was a great privilege to walk out my father's last days with him. As he was dying, he turned to me and said, "Judy, I would not change one thing about my life, it was just right.'"

I can feel his prayers in that heavenly place for us here on earth. Oh Father, I pray that each one of us will realize our journey here on earth is preparation of our mind, heart and spirit to be ready on that last day.

Russell died on March 6th, 1985, and I can hear the voice of our wonderful God saying "well done thou good and faithful servant, you have been faithful over that which is least, now I will make you ruler over that which is much."

John 10:38

Examine my actions and you will see that my work is the work of the Father. Regardless of whether you believe in me - believe the miracles. Then you will know that the Father is in me and I am in the Father. (The Voice)

Chapter 2

Out of the Sea

It happened one day in mid-July. The sun was hot and a warm breeze filled the air. Sherry was turning 16 and it was her heart's desire to celebrate her special day with friends at Half Moon Bay, California. Her parents agreed so 12 of us were off to surf, sand and to have some fun.

Sherry's mother had prepared a banquet for us with all the trimmings of cake, cookies and candies. We teens joined heartily in the feast and after finishing, I ran with my friend Kathy down to the water's edge. Wading out knee-deep, I bent over to wash my hands, all the while talking to Kathy about a new hairdo.

A year earlier there had been a great white shark attack on a couple who had been surfing at this very same beach. The man had lost a leg in the struggle, which canceled my interest in body surfing, as two of my guy friends Rich and Dell were apparently already doing. As I was bent over talking to Kathy, a wall of tsunami-like water swept over us, instantly pulling us both out into the bay with a power I had never felt before. I did have my junior lifesaving certificate so I immediately began to put some of the principles into action.

The loud roar of the waves had not allowed those of us on the beach to hear the cries for help from Rich and Dell. We thought they were just having fun body surfing, but they were caught in a powerful dangerous riptide and were desperately trying to swim to shore. There had been many warnings issued that day on the San Francisco radio stations but we were not from the area and had not tuned into those local stations, thus missing all the warnings.

The power of the waves began to pound down upon me, pushing me well under the surface of the water. I found myself spending all my time just trying to surface and get a breath. The water was so cold it caused an aching and then a numbing feeling. I could not feel my fingers and toes, just my arms and legs. With all this I was rapidly being taken out of the bay beyond the breakers and with no land in sight. I knew I was in serious trouble, and the reality that I just might die was becoming more real than the possibility of surviving. I had a fresh cut on my leg and the fear of attracting a shark was very real.

At this point in my young life I had not talked to the Lord for about two months. I was weary from struggling with the religious to-do's to please my teachers' tyrranical view of God. I didn't want these men and their views of God to come between me and my relationship with my God but it had. I had been sharing a message of salvation by grace in the senior Bible class, and as a result I was removed from running for Student Body Vice President, secretary of my senior class, and song leader. Religious persecution had permeated my senior year and a bitter root was trying to take anchor in my heart.

As these thoughts were running through my mind, I said, "Jesus I have not talked to you for two months and I sure as heck am not going to start crying out for help now that I am in trouble!" I could hear Rick and Dell's cries for help and it reminded me of a movie I had seen of a shipwreck. Their cries sounded surreal as I found myself running out of strength and time. My whole life flashed before me. I was now in my second hour of battling the power of the riptide. I thought, wow, so this is it, just when my mother is beginning to like me and after all the years of trying to raise me right my parents lose me now.

I could see the headlines in the San Francisco paper, "teenage girl drowns at Half Moon Bay." I knew now that I could not get through the waves and back to shore. As the waves pounded me down under the surface they also took me out further each time and now I was beyond the breakers in the open sea. It was at this point that I knew there was nothing left I could do. All my life-saving knowledge was not enough to save me.

I looked up to the heavens and said to the Lord, "there's nothing left I can do Lord. If you see fit to save me, I will serve you." Within moments, I felt something moving me north, parallel with the beach. After 15 minutes or so I began once again swimming toward the shore and this time I was making some real progress. Finally, arriving close to shore but caught in a hole, I saw a man standing about knee-deep to my right. I was too weak to carry on and I yelled out to him for help. As the next wave took me under the surf again, I thought, he thinks I'm kidding as I'm in a hole and he is not! As I surfaced a bit I said, "help, I'm serious, I'm serious, help me!" He came at once and gave me a hand and I walked up onto the beach. It now seemed surreal that I was alive. I could not grasp the truth that I was not going to die. The reality of death for me at this point was more real than the possibility of life and living.

As I looked to my right, I could see way down the beach a group of people gathered around someone. It was too far for me to make out the details and I was too weak to walk the distance. I was afraid someone had not made it. But who? Collapsing down on a sand dune I turned and faced the angry sea and what I saw next changed my life forever.

There were two men stripped down to their skivvies with a rope in their hands that was joined to a lifeguard who was in a pontoon boat with oars wearing a wet suit. The men had tied the rope onto the back of the boat and the lifeguard rowed out to rescue Rick and Dell who were failing fast. He reached them in record time pulling each one into his boat. Then he began his attempt to row back to shore, right where I had just come in. He could not make any headway so he called out to the men who were wading out, rope in hand, to Pull! I watched the two men pull that pontoon boat in against the riptide and thought, if the lifeguard could not row in, how did I swim in?

I knew then that miracles were still happening today. That our wonderful God had not stopped extending his miraculous hand to rescue us. I knew he had sent his angels to rescue me from a circumstance that was bigger than me. I knew I was entering into a deeper relationship with a most loving and forgiving God. A God who wanted to be in a personal relationship with me.

I was beginning to gain some strength, so I stood up, a bit refreshed and started walking towards the crowd who had gathered some distance down the beach. As I drew closer, I could see a man was giving someone mouth-to-mouth resuscitation. Edging in where I could see, I gasped in shock, for there was my friend Kathy! Try though he may, it was too late and I was told later that she had panicked and lost her life in the battle with the sea. I could not believe she was gone. Both of my friends Rick and Dell did live. Rick had taken in too much salt water so he had to spend a few days in the hospital but he recovered fully.

As the rest of us journeyed home that summer day we shared a new resolve to take the fragility of life more seriously. I personally vowed in my heart to press in and reconnect in a deeper way to know my God who had so profoundly rescued me. The very next weekend I had been asked to sing for church. I chose to sing the song "I believe in miracles" and there was hardly a dry eye in the crowd, including mine. What a faithful God we serve.

Ecclesiastes 3:1-4

A time to be born and a time to die, a time to plant and a time to uproot, a time to kill and a time to heal, a time to tear down and a time to build, a time to weep and a time to laugh, a time to mourn and a time to dance, a time to be silent and a time to speak and a time to love. There is a time for everything and the season for every activity under the sun. (NIV)

Chapter 3

Flatlined

At 33 I was living in the Napa Valley of California, famous for their world class wines. I was married to an art professor who was spending many of his out-of-classroom hours portraying the special beauty of this region on canvas. We had three bouncing boys who dotted our lives with joy and ever-unfolding new adventures.

My life had some difficult challenges that I was desperately trying to remedy. My stress level was at an all-time dangerous high, and I was completely unaware of it. Working 10 hour shifts three days a week I was trying to get four days of work crowded into three, as it was my heart to spend more time at home with my family.

One Friday afternoon, my life took a sudden wild turn that forever changed my destiny. It was Memorial Day Weekend and we had decided to take the boys three hours south to their grandparent's home in Watsonville, California, while my husband and I headed on to Carmel to deliver some paintings to the Fireside Gallery. This was my favorite thing to do, and I had entertained some fleeting thoughts during my 10 hour shift that day of a most enjoyable weekend.

  As I arrived home Friday evening I began to feel a great tiredness come over me. So tired that I felt I could not walk up the 32 stairs to reach the front door of our new hillside home. I decided to just sit in the car for a few minutes to catch my breath when suddenly out of nowhere I went into a place of darkness where I knew absolutely nothing. I must have been passed out for a few minutes for when I woke up I was lying across the console and into the passenger seat. I remembered feeling my heart vibrate, rather than beat, before the lights went out. I felt extremely exhausted and didn't know how I was going to climb all those stairs, pack up the boys and take off for a three-hour trip to grandma's house.

  Eventually I ventured out of the car and climbing the first couple of stairs, I found I was short of breath. It stopped me in my tracks. I tried taking some deeper breaths and discovered that if I took three breaths or so I could climb three stairs at a time without stopping. Finally, I reached the front door. Once inside, I decided not to alarm anyone, for with a good night's sleep I was confident I would be fine in the morning. I proceeded to climb another flight of stairs to our bedroom where I packed up a few clothes, and we were off, with all the activities of three very active young boys sitting in the back seat for the next three hours.

The next morning, I tried to rise and shine, but I found the energy it took to just get dressed and ready for the day was completely exhausting. I had to lie down, like it or not. Sunday morning, after a day of rest, I was not much better, and on Monday morning we were heading back home. I had booked three consecutive two-hour appointments for Tuesday morning and after finishing the first one, the last two appointments canceled leaving the afternoon appointments in place but now with a four-hour gap. In my boredom, I decided to walk across the street to the St. Helena Hospital and see Dr. White, who was a wonderful cardiologist and the husband of a dear friend. As Dr. White began to check me over, he turned a little pale and said, "You, lady are going into the hospital. I don't like what I'm hearing."

I canceled my appointments for the remainder of the day and found myself in a hospital bed within an hour. Surprised, I called my husband to let him know I would not be coming home for a few days, and shared the doctor's concerns with him. After three days of monitors, echocardiograms and other tests, Dr. White came into my room and said, "you went into cardiac arrest and I don't know why you're still here. When your heart vibrated it was tired and you flatlined. You needed an electric shock treatment to regenerate your heart to beat again. It's not possible for the heart to restart at that point of exhaustion without electrical stimulation."

Then he proceeded to tell me that our emergency room doctor, Dr. Novak, had the same type of tachycardia, and he had flatlined two months ago, dying on the tennis courts. "Only God knows why *you* are still here." I was suffering from a complete mitral valve prolapse and the life-threatening arrhythmias that accompany 2% of its victims. There was no cure at this time for my condition and they put me on 80mg of Inderal per day, trying to stabilize the arrhythmias.

I was then assigned to my bed for six months of complete rest. I was devastated and could not imagine spending six months in bed with a brand-new home, bills to pay, and three young sons to care for. But there really was no choice as I was now too weak to navigate and was flat on my back. Lying in bed, looking up at the ceiling, a new truth begin to dawn.

My four-year-old was running loose downstairs and I discovered the most amazing thing. When I could do nothing but pray, the Lord would step in and fully take care of whatever concerned me at the moment. I needed to sell my car for instance, and he brought someone to my door who bought it right away. The same thing happened with my grand piano. People came, bought it and took it away. I was just praying and the Lord was doing all the work. The power of prayer became a new reality. A much needed one, as I had totally burned myself out trying to remedy all of my issues and the issues of those closest to me.

I came very close to dying in my car that day in more ways than one. Physically, short of the Lord sending an angel to wake me up, life was over for me at 33. My life was also spiritually compromised as well, as I tried to fix everyone's problems through my own good ideas, fully eclipsing the Lord's best.

Fear began to grip me in a new and powerful way as the medication did not quite cover my arrhythmia problems and my heart would beat erratically as I tried to quiet down for a night's sleep. I didn't know for 18 long years when I went to sleep at night if I would wake up the next morning. For two years I went through the trauma of trying to go to sleep each night and stay asleep without jerking awake. One day it suddenly occurred to me that if the Lord woke me up that afternoon in the car, he and he alone was in charge of when I lived and when I died. Another reality began to dawn: He wasn't through with me yet. He alone was in control of my destiny.

All fear of dying left that day and to this day I have no fear of dying; for I know he is the author of my living and my dying, and when my day is done it will be just right. The doors to my old life had closed in the last six months and God was about to open a brand-new door that would bring three times the blessings of my former life.

One of my clients who had a group home for girls in our area came to me one day and said, "Judy, I've always loved your creative suggestions in dealing with my kids. Would you consider taking one of my girls?" I was totally surprised and took the idea to the Lord to see if it was His. I felt it was and it was the beginning of a whole new life. I loved it. I could make a difference in these girls lives and yet be at home with my boys at the same time. The program went so well that the State came in and asked if they could license me. Five years after I had established the group home in California I was asked by the State of New Hampshire to come there and establish group homes for their state. This I did, providing homes vs. boarding schools for children who were wards of the court. This was a blessing to them as well as to me and my family.

Two foundational truths I learned during this experience. First, if we release all control to our Heavenly Father, he will then take control of our circumstances and orchestrate an outcome that we could never imagine or arrange for ourselves. Secondly, if we pray, wait, and listen, the power we lack to bring the necessary changes in our lives God is ever ready and able to supply if we will lift up our circumstances and release the outcome to him.

John 10:27-29

(Jesus:) My sheep listen to my voice; I know them, and they follow me. I give them eternal life, and they shall never perish; no one will snatch them out of my hand. My Father, who has given them to me, is greater than all; no one can snatch them out of my Father's hand. (NIV)

Chapter 4

Audible Voice of God

Nobody knows the trouble I've seen. Nobody knows but Jesus and so the song goes. It was January, 1997. I had been suffering 18 long years with a severely prolapsed mitral valve, along with a serious arrhythmia. It was responsible for my near-death experience in 1979.

It was customary for me to book an appointment for a yearly check-up with a well-known cardiologist in the Napa Valley, Dr. Peter Van den Hoven. The appointment was set for January 3rd. When that day came, he seemed delighted to see me and he proceeded to run me through an hour and a half of testing (EKG, treadmill, echocardiogram, etc). When the exam was complete he asked me to meet him back in his office.

As I entered his office, I noticed a look of concern on his face as he proceeded to say, "Judy the electrical system of your heart is failing fast, and I want to send you to an expert cardiologist in Sacramento, California, who specializes in pacemakers and defibrillators. I'm recommending that you book an appointment as soon as possible."

I thought, wow, I just don't have time for all this. I stood up, looking at him with surprise and thanked him for his concerns. As I walked out of his office and down a long hallway, I lifted my hands towards heaven and declared: "Heavenly Father, you are in charge of when I live and when I die. I'm putting this in your hands."

Several months flew by and now it was April. I was actively involved in a local prayer ministry where we had been discussing some negative rumors about a pastor who was in the healing ministry. We were wondering if he was legitimate or not. Was he called and anointed by God, or was this just all about him? I decided I had to know, so I called a friend to join my son and I, and on April 17th we were off to Sacramento to check him out.

The Arco Arena was the chosen place for this event. It contained 32,000 seats and it was a packed house that day. The lines were long and it took us well over an hour to get inside the door. Once inside, we could hear the music playing, and for 3 hours we sang praise and worship songs to the Lord.

Finally, the pastor came out. Standing at the podium, he shared with us that he had been in prayer with the Lord for five hours and was just now released to come out and minister to us. So far I was very impressed with the one hundred percent focus on the praise and worship of Jesus. I could find no fault in this man. I saw no narcissistic focus on himself. It was truly his heart to glorify God. After reading some scriptures and opening with prayer, he asked everyone in the room to lay hands on their own body, wherever they were hurting or sick, and he would pray a healing prayer for us all.

I stopped for a moment and thought, then proceeded to lay my right hand on my heart and say to the Lord, "Lord if you choose to heal me, I could better serve you." It was extremely quiet for a few moments and then then the pastor said, "someone has been healed of mitral valve prolapse and the arrhythmias that go with it." I thought oh wow, that sounds like me! But then I thought, Judy, there's 32,000 people here and I quickly dismissed the idea.

Several more months went by and now it was Christmas. There was no snow to be found in all of California that year, so my husband and I decided to take our son Todd and a friend to Sun Valley, Idaho for the holiday.

Large snowflakes were falling on our windshield as we entered Idaho, forming beautiful lacy patterns. We were entering into a winter wonderland, with Christmas lights everywhere. The lodge was large and beautifully appointed. The food was delicious and through the windows we could see the mountains with the fresh fallen snow.

I was growing envious of our young guys flying down those hills all day long without a care in the world. The severity of my heart condition had greatly limited me in regards to physical activity. I was unable to participate in sports or household chores such as vacuuming, scrubbing floors, and running up and down stairs. Anything that would cause the blood to rush through my heart was out.

But I had noticed that I was feeling stronger lately so by the third day I suggested to Wayne that maybe we could try some cross country skiing. It sounded so good, as the woods were incredibly beautiful in this region. The branches were laden with fresh fallen snow; sunlight filtering down. The setting was beyond words. It was majestic to behold. So on this afternoon we decided to take off and find some cross country trails. It didn't take long.

We found a wonderful rustic lodge just down the road and we were out on the trails in no time. The silence that the woods exuded that day was truly inspirational. God was in this place. I could tangibly feel his peace. Wayne and I were having the time of our lives and were sorry to see the sun starting to drop in the western sky. I said to Wayne, I had better not push it. Let's head back to the lodge and call it a day.

As I was skiing down the last hill and over a bridge with a beautiful stream running underneath, I heard a voice speak, a rich baritone voice with a Hebrew accent that said, "Behold, I make all things new." This voice sounded like a voice speaking over many waters. I remembered that scripture and I was thrilled and amazed all at the same time.

I went into the lodge to return my skis and the lady behind the desk looked at me and asked, "are you sure you have never cross country skied before?" I said, "no, this is my first time." She said, "nobody stays out longer than an hour and a half on their first time out. Are you aware that you've been out there for three hours?" I looked at her for a long time and then I thought, heavenly Father you have healed me. I have a brand new heart!

We headed back to the Napa Valley as it was now January and time to make my yearly appointment with Dr. Van den Hoven. I didn't waste any time. I'll never forget walking into his office on that Tuesday morning, when he asked me how things had worked out with the Sacramento cardiology team. I had to admit to him I had not made the call. He looked at me quizzically and said, "well let's take a look." He proceeded to run me through a gamut of tests and then he asked me to join him in the office.

He was sitting in a comfortable chair behind his desk staring at me as I walked in. I was bursting with joy and simply blurted out, "Dr. Van den Hoven, the Lord has healed me. I believe he has given me a new heart!" He leaned even farther back in his chair pausing for a moment then he replied, "well, I do believe he has!" He could find nothing wrong with my heart's electrical system. It was perfect, and the mitral valve was completely healed and functioning normally. I left his office praising the Lord and offering myself up for whatever God had in store for me. I knew I had been prepared to walk it out.

I now was convinced beyond a shadow of a doubt that the Lord is truly in control of when we live and when we die. That maybe it is His desire even more than ours that we finish our journey here on earth according to His sovereign plans. For is there anyone who can take our place? I venture to say, the answer is no!

John 14:13

Whatever you ask for in my name, I will do it so that the father will get glory from the son. Let me say it again: if you ask for anything in my name I will do it. (The Voice)

Genesis 1:26

(God:) Now let us create a new creation, humanity, made in our image, fashioned according to our likeness. And let us grant them authority over all the earth that they may rule over the earth and subdue it. (The Voice)

Chapter 5

Black Flies of Canada

Have you ever wondered how we might be able to walk in God's beautiful creation and escape some of the attacks that often happen there? This is an experience where our wonderful God, creator of it all, answers that question.

My husband and I decided to take our family on a trip to Kelowna, British Columbia, where I would be attending a conference for 30 days through the month of July. The housing situation was tight and everything that was available for families seemed to be already taken. I called the head office, asking if there were any other possibilities. They said they would check around and see. I sent up a quick prayer request and waited. The next morning, I received a call saying there was a women in the area who was offering her 1927 restored log home for the month. I thought wow, too good to be true, as I loved early American history and had always dreamed of one day owning a log home.

We quickly sent in our application and, much to our surprise, our gracious host accepted all four of us. The holiday was on, and we were all in a buzz about it. It was love at first sight, as we rounded the bend and laid our eyes on the most beautiful little valley with its gardens, log home and small river running through the woods. With the help of our wonderful host it didn't take long for us to settle in and get comfortable.

The first morning I woke up with the dawn at about 5:30. I thought wow, wouldn't it be fun to pray out on that old log I had seen yesterday that was leaning out over the water. I had heard horror stories about clouds of black flies that descended upon campers, seriously biting them, and that it took up to three weeks for the intense itching to stop. I found my Cutters bug repellent and lavished it on from head to toe. Grabbing my Bible, I set out with great anticipation for a special time with my God in His beautiful creation. I must say it was everything I thought it would be, including the black flies swarming in a cloud over my head.

The next morning, I awoke about the same time and was very anxious to experience more of this awe-inspiring place. I quietly sneaked out of our room, and as I grabbed the can of repellent on my way out I heard the Lord ask, "Judy. would you trust me this morning to be your covering?" I was surprised to say the least and I definitely needed to think about it for a minute or two. Then, deciding to trust him, I ventured out, taking a detour into the beautiful flower garden on the edge of the woods, just to see how things went.

As I was quietly sitting there, I suddenly heard a panting and running behind me in the woods. It went on for five or so minutes, back and forth, and then I saw him, a magnificent mule buck running across the path that lead down to the river. I jumped up, inspired to move out of my comfort zone, and headed towards the woods. As I neared the edge of the woods, I asked, the Lord, "how can I pray?" The impression came quickly, "Rebuke the spirit of attack in the black flies and mosquitoes in my name, and say they may not bite me and then speak my peace into them."

Quickly praying the prayer, I ran down to the water's edge just in time to see this gorgeous buck run across the stream to join his bride on the other side. I was reminded of the song, "as the deer panteth for the waters so my soul longeth after thee." This morning seemed perfect with the black flies and mosquitoes keeping their distance as I was sitting there in the wonder of it all.

For 28 days this was our morning ritual as I worshiped Him in the beauty of His creation, and He covered me.

On the morning of the 29th day, towards the end of our time together, out of nowhere I received a bite on my neck. I was so surprised that I said, "how dare you bite me after all this time!"

I asked the Lord, "what is this all about," and

He said, "place your hand on the bite and say, be well, in the name of Jesus." So I did, and the bite immediately disappeared. I thought wow, that was interesting!

I gathered up my things, leaving my favorite log, and entered the woods. While I was grieving the loss of this special place, as tomorrow would be my last day here, I suddenly saw a picture of the apostle Paul after the shipwreck, on the island of Cyprus; he was placing wood on the fire when suddenly a black viper struck his hand. I could see several men standing around watching him, expecting him to die. As they watched, he placed his other hand over the bite and said, "BE WELL, in the name of Jesus, BE WELL!"

I knew then, that when we walk by faith with our Lord and Savior Jesus Christ, that He is our ever present, still loving God who covers us with his miraculous hand. Might we awaken to the "MORE" that He has for each one of us, as we seek to know Him more today than yesterday.

John 14:11-12

(Jesus:) Accept these truths; I am in the Father, and the Father is in me. If you have trouble believing based on my words, believe because of the things I have done. I tell you the truth: whoever believes in me will be able to do what I have done, but they will do even greater things, because I will return to be with the Father. (The Voice)

Chapter 6

Africa Bound

The House of Prayer had been especially busy. I was feeling the need for a change when the phone rang. A wonderful doctor and his wife in our community were planning a missions trip to Mozambique, Africa. The mission compound was on the outskirts of the capital city of Maputo and had been established by Heidi and Rolland Baker with a special focus on the orphans of this war-torn nation. My heart leapt with joy for the opportunity to spend some ministry time there.

Dr. Steve extended an invitation to me to join them on this wonderful adventure. My heart sank, for I was contributing heavily of time and money to my House of Prayer and the community there at large. So I said, Steve let me pray about it and I'll get back to you.

The House of Prayer had been prospering in every way body, mind, and spirit. I had seen God's hand at work in many lives and knew that I served a God of miracles, and now I was in need of one. So, turning to the Lord, I petitioned him for funds to be

41

able to go on this great adventure with friends and see what He was doing in this war-ravaged nation.

About a week later, after exhausting all my possibility thinking, trying to raise money for the airfare and trip, the phone rang once more. As I said hello, a new voice responded on the other end of the line. It was a woman who lived in Florida that had heard about my ministry. She said that the Lord had moved her heart to contact me and make a donation of $1800 to my ministry, the exact amount needed for the airfare. Hope rose up in my heart once more and I knew that it was the desire of the Lord to bless me with this trip. I was humbled and excited.

It didn't take me long to dial Dr. Steve and share the good news. He was really pleased and began to lay out some to-do's in preparation for the trip. One of the first things on his list were the 13 inoculations that were required for protection from malaria, typhoid and the like in a third world country. I told him I would check in with my local doctor and get that taken care of.

The following day, as my schedule began to lighten up, I headed for the phone to call my physician when once again, that still small voice asked, "Judy would you allow me to be your covering on this trip?" I wondered how that might work with a doctor heading up this mission trip but I felt a strong, overwhelming peace about walking this out in honor of the Lord's desires.

There was a total of three weeks to prepare and finally the day of departure arrived. My husband volunteered to drive me to Dr. Steve's so we packed up the car and off we went with no inoculations in place. Arriving just in time, we saw Dr. Steve at work loading the van. He flashed a smile as he walked towards us picking up some of my things. As he headed back to the van, he suddenly turned around as if he had forgotten something and said, "Oh Judy, did you ever get those inoculations taken care of?" I looked at him, and said, "Dr. Steve, I have to share something with you that I believe the Lord has asked of me..." As I unfolded the story, he looked at me long and hard while I nervously waited for his reply. Finally he spoke and said, "Well, okay, I'll give you a pass."

I had chosen not to say anything to the others, as my time on the river in Canada with the black flies had opened my mind to a new reality. We serve a God who wants to personally protect us from the attacks of the enemy in ways I had never dreamed of.

The flight from San Francisco to Johannesburg was wonderful for it gave us all a chance to connect in a special way in preparation for the mission that lay ahead. We caught a puddle-jumper that flew us into Maputo, Mozambique where our comfort zone was about to drastically change. Upon arrival there was a tall, nice looking young man from Iris

Ministry waiting for us with a flatbed truck, and the adventure was on. The ride on that flatbed truck over the potholed dirt roads of Africa was one I shall not soon forget.

As we drove into the compound the children ran out to greet us with open arms and the most beautiful happy faces you have ever seen. We were instantly in love. These beautiful children were no longer orphaned, but had been rescued by the wonderful hand of God through momma Heidi. There were 450 children who had found a home at this mission station. In the center of the grounds they had built a six-foot wall around a retreat for missionaries who were coming in from all around the world.

We moved our things into the women's cinderblock bunkhouse, then ventured out to the dining room. We were told to bring our own food and that we would each be responsible for our own meals. As we entered the dining room I saw a blackboard on the wall with an invitation to come to a prayer meeting at 8 o'clock that evening. I knew there would be missionaries from around the world there and I was excited to meet them. That evening as we gathered together, the leader announced that three missionaries were deathly sick with malaria and would we please pray for them. As I lifted these missionaries up before our Heavenly Father who is truly our great physician, I felt to call for His healing hand to touch them and to say: Be well in the name of Jesus, be

44

well!

The next morning, they were all three well and back about their heavenly father's business. It was a wonderful miracle that lead to a teaching on how to pray down the attacks of the mosquitoes in the name of Jesus and then speak God's peace into them. There were no more cases of malaria while I was in that special place and all the missionaries were able to soak up the experience, taking it back to their nations around the world.

We are so cherished by a God who loves to miraculously intervene as we subdue the attacks of the enemy through the power of His name, that name given above all names whereby we enter His peace. The peace that passes all understanding.

Matthew 6:13

Lead us not into temptation but deliver us from evil...that we may be blessed by the Lord our God who is our ruler, maker, and friend. (NIV)

"God's love dispels all darkness as we align ourselves with him." JRL

Chapter 7

The Unexpected Hero

Our daughter Tina, who was attending college in Sacramento, California, was turning nineteen, and a whirlwind of preparations were transpiring. Spring was in full bloom and it seemed just right to have an April birthday in the park. As we scurried around preparing to leave, I realized I forgot to get wrapping paper for her gift so I thought, oh well, I'll just pick some up on the way. We loaded the car and headed down the mountainside and through the beautiful Napa Valley. Vineyards were in bloom as well as many fruit trees and our hearts were filled with anticipation for a fun day with family and friends.

As we approached interstate 80 the traffic was heavy and the last thing we wanted to do was pull off to get wrapping paper, but pull off we did. It was a large megastore and the parking lot was full. I hurriedly found what I needed and ran back, laying my wallet on the back bumper of our car, I proceeded to wrap the package right then and there. I was feeling the pressure of the time constraint due to the heavy traffic so I rushed through the wrapping process, and jumped back into the front seat leaving my wallet sitting on the bumper of our car.

We arrived at our destination an hour and a half later. I began gathering my belongings when suddenly the light dawned and I realized what I had done. There was no going back now. The party was on and I needed to stay.

I placed a quick call to the store where I purchased the wrapping paper and reported the lost wallet. They returned the call within an hour and said the wallet had not been turned in yet.

I was now in a bit of panic as in the wallet I had over $100 in cash, plus credit cards and of course all of my ID. I cried out to the Lord to send an angel, asking Him to somehow, someway rest a desire upon the heart of the finder to return my wallet.

Meanwhile, there was a very poor, lonely man who had recently gone through a devastating divorce. His car was so old the paint had worn thin in spots. Broke and penniless, he had been invited by a friend to come and live in one of his bedrooms until he could get back up on his feet. As he was traveling south heading home he noticed the black wallet on the opposite side of the highway heading north. He thought wow, could I ever use some cash. So he made a U-turn as soon as possible and headed north to retrieve the wallet. It had fallen into the center aisle between both north and south lanes and he was actually able to pull over and pick it up. Opening the wallet, he saw the cash but exploring further he also saw my phone number and now the battle was on. The needs were great, but could he spend someone else's money and live with it? In about three hours I received a call and this wonderful man let me know he had found my wallet and that it was in his heart to return it.

He said he was living in a dangerous neighborhood, so he chose to drive quite a few miles out to the highway where he could safely connect with us at a McDonald's. The minute I met this special man I could see the poverty he was suffering from and I was overwhelmed with the "power of God's love" that had so melted this man's heart to do the honest thing. I insisted on a cash reward which he reluctantly accepted, and I was able to pray a blessing over his life. I told him I had prayed, asking God for an angel to protect my wallet and return it to me, and that he had been that "angel" for the Lord that night. He replied, "ma'am, I'm no angel!" And I said, "oh, but you are the one God chose and trusted to pick up my wallet and safely return it to me."

I can only imagine the outpouring of God's blessings that followed this wonderful man after such a heroic choice to do the honest thing.

James 5:16b

The prayer of a righteous person is powerful and effective. (NIV)

Psalms 91:11

For he will command his angels concerning you to guard you in all your ways. (NIV)

Chapter 8

Eric and the Fish Pond

From the flats of Kansas to the hills of Massachusetts, my husband had just accepted a position as chairman of an art department in a small liberal arts college about an hour west of Boston. We were totally captivated by the charm of New England with its historic sites and 18th century architecture. The college had offered us a lovely home situated on campus that we readily accepted and our move was now in full swing.

Our son Eric, who was just two at the time, seemed to be afraid of nothing. I was busy with all that a move entails and it seemed every time I turned around Eric was venturing out into a new danger zone and needed rescuing.

Our new home was situated in the middle of an acre of lawn, with woods to our right and a 19th century mansion beyond. The mansion was four stories high with a large, beautiful leaded glass window that reached from floor to ceiling on the fourth floor. It looked out to the small yard below with woods that bordered our properties.

The college had beautifully restored this

historic home and it now housed the English department. Kurt Ganter, a young, talented professor had recently been asked to chair this department. He readily accepted the position and proceeded to move in, choosing that fourth story room with the leaded glass window for his new office. Pushing his desk up to that window, he could now sit and look out at the beauty of the New England woods where he envisioned himself doing some creative writing.

One of the college policies we all found inviting was the school's closing down for the weekend every Friday at noon. This allowed the professors to be able to go home and prepare for the weekend. Kurt found this very convenient as his little five-year-old son needed to be picked up from kindergarten at noon on Fridays.

What none of us had noticed in the small yard between the woods and the mansion was an old antiquated fishpond, filled with water and lily pads. It was a wonderful haven for frogs and the like, and a playground for my four-year-old and two-year-old sons. From the house I could see the boys in the yard running in and out of the woods with their imaginations in full swing playing their cowboy and Indian games, but I couldn't see the fish pond, so on this particular Friday when I saw them out there, I didn't think much about it.

Kurt was sitting at his desk reading a great book. The Paul Revere bell was ringing from the old church in town indicating it was noon and time to pick up his son from school. The book had captured his attention, and for some reason he decided to stay just a little longer. Meanwhile, my two young sons had discovered the fish pond and were actively trying to catch the frogs as they jumped up on the lily pads. It wasn't long before my little Eric reached out a bit too far for that frog and tumbled head first into the four-foot deep pond.

Kurt said he didn't hear anything. He looked up to find it was now 12:30 and was concerned about the lateness of time. As he stood up he looked out and said his heart nearly stopped as he saw the top of Eric's head in the fish pond! He didn't know how long Eric had been there. All he knew was there were three flights of stairs between him and Eric and he was scared. He flew down those stairs and out to the yard, pulling little Eric up and out of the pond.

The next thing I knew someone was knocking at my door and when I opened the door there was Kurt, holding Eric, dripping in green moss, white as a sheet. I just about died!

We all knew why Kurt stayed overtime that day to read his book. I called the school and told them the story and the fish pond was filled that very afternoon with a load of gravel.

I had been praying that the Lord would watch over my boys, especially Eric, never dreaming of the imminent danger around the corner. We serve   a loving God who hears our prayers; who is ready, willing and most able to honor them.

Matthew 25:23

His master said to him, "Well done, good and faithful servant. You have been faithful over a little; I will set you over much. Enter into the joy of your master." (NIV)

Chapter 9

Faithful in That Which is Least

Colonial Williamsburg had always been a favorite place in my heart as I steward a deep love for American history and how our lives here in this inspiring place began. In 2004 all the doors seemed to open for my husband to establish a career in real estate in this historic place. We were excited. Within two-and-a-half months, our home sold, and off we went with great joy and anticipation. Upon arriving in Williamsburg we were able to secure a special little home overlooking a beautiful setting, and we settled in for a long stay. My husband's new career got off to a great start and everything seemed just right in our world.

One evening around bedtime while I was busy upstairs putting one of the children to bed I heard Wayne call out, saying "Judy, everything's spinning around in the room and I'm not feeling right." I ran down the stairs and into the living room where I found him sitting in a stupor. Somehow I recognized stroke symptoms right away so I called both of our children downstairs and we were able to help him into our car and rush him to the hospital. I ran into the emergency room lobby, grabbed a wheelchair, and hurried out to retrieve my husband.

As I proceeded to wheel him into the emergency room I bypassed the intake nurse at the desk and announced: "My husband's having a stroke" and on I ventured into the treatment room.

They took a look at Wayne and saw immediately what was going on. Whipping into action, they gave him a shot that stopped the stroke. In one hour our lives were permanently changed; our future suddenly unknown. Fear gripped our hearts as we contemplated the outcome. All our dreams were fast melting into nothing.

After a few hours and many tests, they placed Wayne in ICU. I took the kids by the hand and headed home. After tucking the children into bed and assuring them everything was going to be alright I walked into our bedroom crying out to God, what is all this about?

After four days in the hospital, when all the test results were in, the doctor walked into Wayne's room where I was standing and said, "you have a congenital narrowing of the carotid artery in your brain and it is filled with plaque. We cannot stent it. There is nothing more we can do. We recommend that you go home and get your affairs in order. We believe sometime within the next six months you could have the big one and there is nothing that we can do for you because of the location of this plaque."

So it was with sober contemplation that we both drove home that day crying out to the Heavenly Father to show us the way! We pursued a second opinion, but to no avail. The prognosis was the same. So we began a new journey into the unknown, not dreaming of the outcome God had in store for us. Due to the damage caused by this stroke, Wayne was not able to drive. He was experiencing extreme weakness and general instability which of course immediately removed him from the world of real estate. Under these new circumstances we needed to move out of our new home within three weeks into a home we could afford. I turned to the Lord asking, where we should go?

As I pressed for some direction, I felt impressed to go to a real estate agency that handled rentals in town. On the way down I began to hear the name of a street I didn't know existed. When we arrived, walking into the agency I asked them if there was a home for rent on Meadowbrook Drive. The agent looked at me with surprise, and said, "why yes there is. Would you like to see it?" We agreed and off we went.

The house had fallen victim to a hurricane 12 months earlier that had swept through Williamsburg. A tree had fallen on the garage creating a small hole in the roof and many trees on the property next door were down. The German family that had built the home 4 years earlier were overwhelmed by the storm and its damage, so they packed up their family and moved out of state. The home had been empty for over a year and they were very anxious to rent it out.

This 4000 square-foot brick home with two master bedrooms on a beautiful golf course was perfect in every way to meet our needs. They had even lowered the rent, reducing it by 50%. We talked it over with our son and his precious wife who also lived in Williamsburg. They chose to join us and we all moved in together, thus sharing expenses, so we were able to survive and get valuable time to reorganize in the midst of this crisis.

After seven months, it was March, and time for Wayne and I to move on. I was offered a ministry position in Washington, DC. So, packing up our computers, clothes and car we left everything else behind which allowed us to move into a 560 square foot brownstone on 4th Street. It was directly behind the Supreme Court where we could walk to literally everything.

Wayne's health seemed to be slowly improving, so we were encouraged even though our funds would run out by November 1st. This rcmained a nagging concern in the back of our minds.

We were excited to be close to the Capital and all that goes with that world. It was inspiring to have the national museums and capitol in our front yard. But a serious issue began to unfold. The woman who hired me started requiring some unethical compromises, pushing my back up against the wall. I was faced with a choice to compromise my moral values to keep my job, or take a chance on remaining true to my values and have no job. I decided I would rather take a chance on God's provisions and follow an ethical path so the woman moved on, leaving me behind without work.

In about seven days, I accepted an invitation to join the Luis Palau prayer team. Luis Palau was planning a large Youth Festival on the Mall in Washington, DC in August of that year, 2005, and the prayers were greatly needed. I was delighted to join the team as a volunteer. Prayers ascended, and plans were laid. The skateboard props were built and the stages were set in place. Everything was ready to go.

When Saturday morning rolled around we all woke up to a torrential rainstorm outside. Flash floods were upon us with no clear skies in sight. Wayne and I decided not to let this stop us so we went to the prayer tent anyway. When we arrived, there were two other people from different states inside who had decided to do the same thing. We all huddled there in the tent together, in the storm, from 9am to 1pm, praying as the Holy Spirit directed us for the youth of America. Meanwhile the water level on the saturated lawn was rising up above our ankles.

As we closed out our prayer vigil, I turned my attention to the lady sitting next to me. She asked me why I was in Washington and I told her that I believed God wanted me to do a new prayer ministry in the city but I didn't know where yet. She asked me if I knew Bobby Romas and I said no, I hadn't met her. She gave me a phone number and said she thought Bobby might be in town and that she thought she was looking for new directors for her National House of Prayer for The American Christian Trust. She thought we might be a good fit. I took the phone number and putting it into my wallet I said, "Heavenly Father, when you want me to call Bobby Romas you let me know and I will take this number out."

I waited day after day hearing nothing. Seven days went by and one week later the Lord impressed me to get the number out and make the call. When I called, I discovered no one had even been at the Trust to answer the phone anyway, even if I had tried. There was a young couple there from Europe, staying the weekend, so they made the appointment for us on Tuesday morning when Bobby would be returning from Israel. We were excited, wondering what God had in store for us.

Tuesday finally arrived and the meeting with Bobby Romas was wonderful. She said she had wanted to leave early but the Lord impressed her to stay that day for our appointment. It was a divine appointment for sure. She stayed on for several days training us to be the new directors for The American Christian Trust. This house of prayer was birthed during the Reagan years for the White House and also for many Christian leaders who might want to come to DC for a spiritual retreat with their associates.

We moved in one month before our money ran out and prospered in every way you can imagine and beyond. It was truly God's House of Prayer, where we witnessed many ministers with their teams come in discouraged and leave renewed. Churches multiplied, new ministries were birthed, and Wayne was experiencing life extension for the cause of Christ! What might we have missed if we had not been faithful in going down to the prayer tent that stormy day? I shudder to think.

This was only the beginning of Wayne's healing journey, for in 2016 he was called in by his cardiologist to have an angiogram. Before we left the house on the morning of his appointment, we felt impressed to read 2 Kings 20. When we opened our Bible and began to read, we saw God extending the life of Hezekiah after he cried out in prayer for the healing of his life-threatening disease. I sensed the Lord was asking me to pray a life extension prayer for Wayne. So we bowed in prayer, asking our heavenly Father to come in and heal Wayne's vascular system in the name of Jesus.

We arrived at the hospital just in time for the nurse to take Wayne in for the procedure. About an hour-and-a-half later the cardiologist came around the corner of the waiting room and walking toward me with a smile on his face said, "I can't explain it, but I can't find any plaque in Wayne's arteries. They are clear!"

We truly serve a God whose arms are not too short to touch us with His miraculous hands. He so desires to bless us in more ways than we might imagine. Might we all press in for more.

"Oh heavenly Father, you have demonstrated to me that you will be faithfully walking out what concerns me, as I am faithfully walking out what concerns you." JRL

Chapter *10*

Angelic Visitation

It was summertime in Hidden Valley Lake, California. The temperatures outside had been rising to well over 100 degrees and most of us in the neighborhood were retreating into our air-conditioned homes for relief. My friend Jan and I decided to try something new for the summer, and invited some of our neighborhood friends home for a Sabbath lunch and fellowship. We sent out invitations and before we knew it the house was full and buzzing with meaningful conversations and delicious food.

After several weekends had passed one of our children came to us and said, "you know when Billy comes into the house every Saturday morning, he heads straight for our bedroom, opening drawers and closet doors, helping himself to our things without asking. We've talked to him asking him to please ask us first, but he just won't listen to us. He's also throwing a baseball in the family room and we're afraid he's going to break something." I assured him that I would talk with Billy myself and try to curb the problem.

The following week when ten-year-old Billy

came bounding in the front door, I walked down the hall with him. I proceeded to assure him that if he just asked, there would be things he could play with. But I'm afraid Billy blew it off and did as he jolly well pleased once again, much to my chagrin. Now Billy just happened to be the 10-year-old son of my good friend Jan, and the last thing I wanted was to create any hard feelings between us. I decided to take it to the Lord and seek his wisdom on this sensitive matter.

When the next weekend rolled around, the house was once again filled with wonderful conversations, good food and of course Billy on the prowl. As the evening arrived and the guests were gone, I wandered into the kitchen to get a snack. When I walked over to our new table to sit down, there to my horror was Billy's last name carved deeply into the center of its butcher block top. A fear of what might happen next with our loose cannon "Billy" in the house began to rise. I knew I had to do something about it. The time had come to talk with Jan, but as I mulled it over, I couldn't think of any way to present this problem without offending her and disturbing what God was doing in the house with all these beautiful people who were coming each weekend. Once again I brought it back before the Lord, presenting it to him and asking him to intervene somehow someway in this rising problem.

The next morning, we were sleeping in, when

suddenly eight year old Alex came bursting into our room declaring "there is a light in the kitchen bay window --- come quick." We all ran out to the kitchen only to find the light was gone, but as we looked down at the kitchen table, Billy's last name was perfectly removed and the butcher block table top looked brand new once again!

We all stood there looking at the table and each other in amazement, realizing that the light in the kitchen had been an angel that was sent to heal a most difficult situation. Our fears dissipated as we realized that not only was Billy in the hands of God, but so was our home.

We saw a new aspect of our loving Savior that day who cares about the little things in our lives enough to send an angel to repair a kitchen table top.

P.S. The miracle table was later given to an international mission bungalow in Washington, DC where the story lives on.

Psalms 23:2-4

He provides me rest in rich, green fields besides streams of refreshing water. He soothes my fears; He makes me whole again, steering me off worn, hard paths to roads where truth and righteousness echo His name. (The Voice)

Chapter *11*

God's Divorce Recovery

New Year's day had arrived and all was not well in the house. I found myself sitting on the couch looking out at the view, wondering what my future would hold in the coming year.

After 25 years of marriage my husband packed up his things and left the house, stepping into what he thought was a greener pasture. The house was empty, the children were gone, and a feeling began to sweep over me of great aloneness. The sun was shining sweetly across the hills and yet I could not feel its warmth. It was as if a cloud of darkness was engulfing my world. A true sense of hopelessness began to fill my thoughts; tears filled my eyes.

I began crying out to God, declaring, I tried it all God, twenty-five years of marriage including seven years of counseling, but to no avail. Why had things gone so wrong, I asked him. I felt completely defeated and utterly unhappy. Any thought tunnel I looked into seemed to have no light at its end. Starting the new year without my family together in the house was more than I could bear. I was desperate to find relief from this loneliness. Oh God, come and take me out of this dark place, I cried.

Suddenly a white light filled one corner of the room and I began to feel a sense of peace. I didn't move; I just sat there soaking in it. Feelings of hope began to sweep over me and the feelings of despair began to lift. As I sat there in this angelic presence, an impression came to call an old friend who also had fought for her marriage and lost.

This presence of the Lord was changing the atmosphere of my home and my mind. I no longer felt alone but knew that my God was with me. The deep grief of the loss of my marriage began to lift, and hope began to fill my mind and heart once again.

After about 25 minutes the angelic presence slowly left the room. I got up off the couch looking for the phone to connect with my friend. I was able to reach her right away and as we shared our experiences together on that New Year's Day, I was greatly encouraged and began to look forward to the new year that lay ahead.

This was a profound, life-changing experience. I discovered that when we soak in our circumstances rather than the presence of our wonderful God, darkness will engulf us. Worry, fear and a feeling of aloneness will stream into our minds, hearts and spirits, taking up residence, so to speak. I realized that re-running negative thoughts only took me down into a hole of depression, and that when

I reached up for the Lord's wonderful light he was more than ready, willing, and most able to supply it.

I would encourage all who are reading this story right now to stop and pray, giving your difficult situation over to our wonderful God who knows your pain and has the solution if you seek him for it. He never said there'd only be rainbows. He never said there'd be no rain. He only promises a heart full of singing in the very things that once brought pain, and so the song goes: "Give it all, Give it all, Give it all to Jesus."

PS. I asked the Lord that day to bring me the man of His choice as I hadn't done such a good job choosing the first one. He did just that, as I trusted Him and allowed Him to take the lead. I have been very happily married for some years now and many of my heart's desires for the first marriage are now present in my second. We serve a God who is a most present help in times of trouble.

Psalms 32:7-8

You are my hiding place, you will keep me out of trouble and envelop me with songs of deliverance. You will teach me and tell me the way to go and how to get there. You will give me good counsel and you will watch over me. (The Voice)

Chapter *12*

Miracle of the Heart

I'm sure on some level we can all identify with the phrase, "Experience is often the best teacher." Well, as I reflect back on my earlier years of growing up I can see this principle being applied through the wisdom of my Dad. He was always standing close by to rescue me if needed but, more often than not, he would wisely guide me through current difficult circumstances rather than prematurely rescuing, as he saw it.

One autumn morning in our mountaintop home in Northern California, while my Dad was in class and my mother in the kitchen, I ventured outside to find something fun to do. I was three-and-a-half at the time and there were some real dangers around our mountain home that I was unaware of. My mother had asked my father to build a picket fence around the front lawn he had recently planted to keep me contained, and that he did, painting it white to please her.

On this particular morning, while I was playing in my favorite dress in the yard, I looked up, and for the first time, I noticed an oak tree 30 feet or so beyond the fence. I began to wonder what I might be able to see from the top. Climbing up and over the fence, catching my hem on a picket, I was off to explore. I took my time as this oak tree was the largest in our neighborhood and definitely a challenge. As I ventured toward the top the view was spectacular and I was thrilled. I could see the farm with all the cows and sheep in the pasture, and the homes around ours with my friends playing in their yards.

It was wonderful until I looked down and asked myself how do I get back down from here? A feeling of fear gripped me and I began to call out to my mother for help. She came running out of the house and just about died when she saw me stuck at the top of the tallest tree in our neighborhood. She ran into the house and called the school, asking them to find my Dad, who was in class, and send him home quickly.

She was so scared she stayed in the house and I just stood there on one of those top branches waiting for my daddy's rescue. I knew if he was coming everything was going to be just fine and I resumed enjoying the view. It must have been about twelve to fifteen minutes for all the connections to be made along with my Daddy's trip up the hill to our home.

When my Dad arrived he ran over to the tree and looking up he said, "well, Judy, I can see you're going to be climbing this tree, so let me show you how to do it." I was most happy. His choice was not to rescue me but instead he climbed up the tree to where I was and then showed me how to climb back down, leading me out of my dilemma.

I learned to face a challenge without fear that day as my father walked it out with me. This was just the beginning of many adventures with my father who was my mentor and a great source of wisdom for so many of life's challenges.

When he reached age 62 he suddenly contracted a type of cancer for which there was no cure. Once again, I saw this wise man rise up in his hospital bed to share with Loma Linda University medical students what life was like on the other side of knowing there is no cure for you and that the end is near.

It was my desire to stand beside my father during his last few days, so I flew out to California from New Hampshire, leaving the care of the children with my husband who was an artist in residence at the time, on our farm.

As I was watching my father's life ebb away I received a call from my husband who didn't feel he could watch the children any longer, as he wanted more time to paint. It was hard to leave before my father was at rest as when he would wake out of his coma he would call out my name. Thirty hours after I arrived back home I received the call that he was gone. I was so upset that I couldn't be there for him as he had always been there for me. I went out to my car while the kids were in school and drove to a beautiful lake, with about two feet of snow on the ground. As I sat there in tears realizing my mentor was gone a voice spoke to me and said, "Judy, would you consider turning your grief into celebration for the wonderful father I gave you?" I thought about the gift of this special human being who always seemed to be there with wise counsel and I said, yes, I will give you my grief in exchange for celebration.

I don't know how our wonderful God and now my mentor did it, for there is no way I can explain what happened next. I suddenly felt a feeling of GREAT JOY as I began to recount the life experiences my father had so faithfully and wisely walked through with me. My heart was forever transformed that day as my Heavenly Father walked through my greatest loss with me, miraculously exchanging grief for "Celebration!"

The tears are gone and I am still celebrating to this day. Might we take a look at our circumstances that are before us today as an opportunity to invite the "Mentor" of all mentors into our daily lives, to upgrade our relationship with Him? That we might live with Him in a place of peace, joy and love. I believe this is one of the top 10 great desires of our Lord's heart!

Joel 2:30

I will give signs of my intervention; to all who call upon the name of the Lord they will be liberated. (The Voice)

Chapter 13

A Sign and Wonder

It was Saturday night and the party was definitely on. With great excitement my 15-year old son Todd and I were preparing to meet up with friends we hadn't seen for ten years. A birthday dinner for the hostess was planned for 6:30 pm and everyone was able to make it. The time seemed to just fly by as we all told our stories and got caught up on what was new. Before we knew it, it was midnight and we realized we were an hour-and-a-half from home. Hugging everyone goodbye, we rushed out to our car, chatting about the night's conversations; climbing into our little Honda hatchback we buckled up and were off to Huntington Beach.

We drove onto the 55 freeway and pulled into the fast lane. The traffic seemed especially thick for that time of night. I decided to pull out of the fast lane on this eight-lane highway and stay in the lane to the right of it. I was traveling about 75 miles an hour when all of a sudden a dark mass ran into my left door and headlight. There was no time to even think about touching the brakes or controlling the wheel as the impact was causing the wheel to spin out of control thus taking us across three lanes of traffic right into a concrete wall.

The next thing I knew, as I was regaining consciousness, was that the car was spinning on two wheels circling right in rotations going down the highway hitting the concrete wall with every rotation. The force of gravity was so great I remember thinking it felt like a Disneyland ride and I realized we were in a major crash. I reached my right arm over in a panic to the passenger seat, wondering if my son Todd was still there and he was, thank God!

We hit the wall again still on two wheels with a force of gravity laying us down in our seats. Then I thought, if I just lay my right foot slowly on the brake, it might bring us back down on all four wheels. So I proceeded to try it and sure enough it worked. As the car came to a bouncing halt, we were suddenly facing a highway packed with lights all shining directly at us. We were in shock that no one had hit us!

A young man of about 35 jumped out of his car and came running up to us, asking if we were okay and I said, "I think so." Then he said, "there is a God, there is a God, I now know there is a God!" He said, "there is no way you could have stayed on those two wheels for all those rotations hitting the concrete wall without rolling over and over and over down the highway!"

We were pinned inside the car, unable to safely get out. Looking in my rearview mirror I could see a white maxi truck and I knew that was the truck that had hit us. I saw a man getting out having difficulty walking a straight line as he headed toward us.

I tried to lower my window but it would not drop more than two inches due to the damage. As he approached my window he said he had fallen asleep at the wheel and had forgotten to turn on his lights. His breath reeked of alcohol. I knew I needed to detain him until the police arrived so, I struck up a conversation to keep him engaged.

Other people began to get out of their cars to see if we were okay and to let us know they had notified the police. Not only were they amazed that we had lived through this major crash, but both highway patrolmen who arrived on the scene told us the same thing. We were truly the Lord's "sign and wonder" on the 55 freeway at 1:00 am that Sunday morning. The car was totaled but we walked away with barely a scratch on us.

What was so amazing to my son and I is when we left our friends and got into the car we had fastened our seat belts when our minds were so preoccupied with sharing the night's events. Neither one of us used our seat belts on a regular basis.

The rescue that night by the Lord's angel who took the wheel was a sign and wonder to all who witnessed it, and a visual testimony of the Lords loving care in the midst of danger.

Psalms 31:14-20

But I trust in you, Lord, I say, "you are my God." My times are in your hands; deliver me from the hands of my enemies, from those who pursue me. Let your face shine on your servant; save me in your unfailing love. Let me not be put to shame, Lord, for I have cried out to you; but let the wicked be put to shame and be silent in the realm of the dead, let their lying lips be silenced for with pride and contempt they speak arrogantly against the righteous. How abundant are the good things you have stored up for those who fear you, that you bestow in the sight of all, on those who take refuge in you. In the shelter of your presence you hide them from all human intrigues; you keep them safe in your dwelling from all accusing tongues. (NIV)

Chapter 14

Confrontation in the Hood

My husband and I were finally settled into our new home in Southern California, about three miles from the ocean. We were enjoying the cool breezes that blew in every evening as we walked the cliff-lined beaches nearby. Our children had all left home, opening precious time for Wayne and I to travel, explore some new sights, and write.

Our grandson had called about a month earlier from Northern California to share his dream of how he wanted to work his way through college as a waiter in one of the finer restaurants in the Napa Valley. We loved his plan and wanted to help if needed. He was without a car at the time so we decided to give him a hand up and supply the car, allowing his dream to become a reality.

Because of our recent move we were still unfamiliar with some of the towns and neighborhoods of Southern California. As we scanned Craigslist our eyes fell upon an ad for the car of our choice which just happened to be in LA County. We had high hopes as we had been looking for a while, but to no avail. We googled the address into our GPS and we were off once more to parts unknown. We took several thousand dollars in cash with us, hoping to better our chances for a more competitive price. Approaching an hour and a half on the unfamiliar LA freeway we finally reached our destination.

As we entered into the neighborhood we noticed bars on all of the windows. There was a small Rocky Balboa Boxing gym on our left with a boarded up church and yard just beyond.

I noticed two men standing in one of the small chain-link fenced yards on my right and I got an uneasy feeling about them. The first man was very large and reminded me of Hoss from the old Bonanza series on TV. The second man was very small and was moving in slow-motion as if high on something.

My husband parked three doors down on their side of the street and said to me, "you had better wait in the car, but I've driven an hour-and-a-half to see this car so I at least want to see it before we leave." He stepped out, taking the keys with him and proceeded to cross the street, walking down past the church and around the corner into its parking lot.

As I watched my husband go out of sight, I looked up in my rearview mirror to see Hoss leave his yard, and he was heading straight for me! I knew instantly I was in trouble and I cried out to the Lord for help. I felt impressed to get out, leave the cash inside and lock the car. As I started walking across the street towards the church I begin to pray out loud, "Heavenly Father I rebuke the strategic plans of the enemy to harm me, in Jesus name, and I call forth your angels to come guard and protect me."

I sensed Hoss was gaining on me and a chill ran up my spine as I turned around to see where he was, and there he stood, not three feet from me pointing a pistol straight at my chest. He said, "Missy are you lost?" I instantly felt a courage I had not known before fill me and I looked him straight in the eye and said "NO, I'm not lost!"

Hoss paused, and after looking at me for a few long moments, he turned right and made a large half circle away from me. Crossing the street, he headed toward town.

I had to smile to myself as I watched this 300-pound man so quickly trying to escape my 115-pound presence. I don't know if Hoss saw angels or just felt the powerful presence of the Lord that day, but I do know, it was an encounter of the living Christ, on the sidewalk that day, in front of the boarded up church in the hood.

Psalms 27:8-11

My heart says of you, "seek His face!" Your face Lord I will seek. Do not hide your face from me. Oh Lord you have been my helper!.. Teach me your way. Oh Lord, lead me in your straight path. (NIV)

Chapter *15*

Flying High in the Backseat

Now, I don't know about you, but the back seat of a plane is "NOT" where I want to spend six hours, propped up like a mannequin sitting next to the latrine. If truth be known, I have created a bit of a fuss when my seat has suddenly been changed to this uncomfortable zone.

At the beginning of the summer of 2015 I was feeling the need for a break as I had been on the fast track all spring. A trip to the East Coast was long overdue. I had not seen my oldest and dearest friend from New England for several years and decided this was the perfect time. So, the plans were laid, and I was off to a much overdue reunion, an experience that one can only have with that special person who comes along early in our lives who weathers our ups and downs and in-betweens for the rest of our lives

I decided to book a flight that would include both of our birthdays along with getaways such as Old Alexandria, Virginia. I also booked a seat in row 7A, a window seat as I so love to sit in that quiet inspiring space with the ever-changing scenery passing below. Truly a place removed from the pace of everyday life, where one could contemplate and write creative new thoughts. During the hustle and bustle preceding the trip I found myself dreaming of sitting in that window seat.

Finally, the day arrived, and I was off to battle the crowds at LAX. The lines at the airport were long and I was relieved when I finally reached the front desk to get the printout of my ticket. Grabbing the handle of my carry-on, I started walking towards the security check-in when I noticed that my seat had been changed to number 36B. I paused and thought, that's odd, but I guess I'll wait and see what it looks like, so I continued on toward the gate. Boarding the plane, I entered first class and as I looked down the aisle in front of me, my heart began to sink. Were there even 36 rows of seats on this plane, I wondered, and if so, might 36B be on the aisle in the last row by the latrine?

Sure enough there it was - the worst seat in the back of this Airbus, assigned to me. My mind began to whirl with the injustice of it all for hadn't I booked seat 7A in advance? Who had changed my seat assignment and why? I put my carry-on in the overhead and sat down in this most erect seat backed up against the wall. I decided there had been a great mistake and I needed to call for the attendant to get this matter straightened out.

As I looked up to find the attendant button, I heard the still small voice whisper, "really Judy, someone has to sit in this seat, why not you?" I recognized the still small voice only too well, and I knew what I needed to do, all the while everything in me was screaming out with disappointment, for the plans and dreams that were made had somehow been changed.

As I look back at that place in time, I shudder to think of the divine purposes of God that might have been eclipsed that day had I tried to reclaim my original seat. Little did I know that it was the Lord who had changed my seat, and a divine appointment was in the making.

As we took off, climbing up above the clouds, everything seemed quite normal and in place. Once we had reached our designated altitude I turned to my seat mate and introduced myself. We were engaged in conversation when all of a sudden a commotion broke out in front of us. I heard a woman speaking to her husband, trying to wake him. Looking over the back of their seats I saw a man of about 60 years of age in a slump, unconscious, not responding to his wife's probes. I sat back down on my seat asking, Lord how shall I pray? He said, "he's having a stroke and he doesn't know me. I want you to ask the Father for life extension and healing."

So I did. I cried out to God to give this man a second chance; to get to know his Creator as Lord and Savior, a living God who so desired to become his friend.

An attendant showed up and began asking through the intercom if there was a doctor or nurse in the house. All the while I continued to pray. Within about four minutes the man suddenly sat up and looked around as a nurse arrived and took his vitals. Within minutes this man who had been unconscious was looking perfectly normal and was asking questions! The nurse chose to sit in the middle seat between the husband and wife for the rest of the trip even though all seemed well, just to keep an eye on him. Then the Lord spoke to me again and said "I want them to know about the prayer I gave you. I want him to know that I have something special for him should he so desire to seek me for it."

So, I got up out of my seat and kneeling beside his wife, I proceeded to speak to the man at the window who seemed very interested in what I had to say. I shared with him the healing prayer that the Lord had given me. Then, finished with the Lord's invitation to seek Him, I taught them both how to pray, then wait and listen for the Lord's reply. As we continued, they said they used to be Christians but had drifted into their own lives leaving spiritual pursuits behind. They seemed very moved and hungry to seek the Lord, and thanked me profusely for my prayer and ministry to them.

As I sat back down in seat 36B I realized my

life had taken on a whole new dimension, a new dimension with my wonderful God. Had I missed anything? I dare say not; not a thing. I had the pleasure of partnering in prayer with our wonderful Savior, the God of the second chance, who longs to be in friendship with us.

Jeremiah 29:11-13

For I know the plans I have for you, says the Lord. Plans to give you hope and a future. Then you will call on me and pray to me and I will listen to you. You will seek me and find me when you seek me with all your heart. I will be found by you. (NIV)

Chapter *16*

Cancer at My Door

Time seemed to be advancing at a rapid pace. My husband and I were becoming increasingly concerned, actually alarmed, over the fast paced atmosphere surrounding our young boys in California. Pulling up stakes we found ourselves on our way to a charming New England town that was rich in our American heritage and values. Purchasing a beautifully restored New England farm on eight wonderful acres it was truly a new beginning for us all. My husband, who was chairman of an art department in a local liberal arts college in California, had chosen to resign his position and step out into the world of fine art. He had a very good reputation as a landscape artist and was encouraged by his mentor to make a run for it.

I, on the other hand, had developed a very fine program for Small Family Group Homes in the State of California. I decided to present my program to the state of New Hampshire where the concept of Small Family Group Homes had not been realized yet. They welcomed my program and found funding for it right away through three wealthy families who had a passion to see children who were abandoned thrive in their communities.

I specialized in girls between the ages of four and seventeen, which provided a comfortable space between their program and that of my sons. I bought a New England farm with eight acres and with this all in place, we were off to a roaring start. Summertime had arrived. In the lower field my sons were busy building jumps for their dirt bikes; in the second floor studio my husband was painting the beautiful New England landscape; and the girls were off with their horses in the corral. There seemed to be inspiration and yet challenges for all. It was truly a summer to remember.

One day in early October, I received a call from my mother who told me my father was in the hospital due to some intense pain he had been experiencing in his abdomen. She said they were going to run a myriad of tests to try and identify the source of the pain. I was immediately alarmed as my father had always been an anchor in my life and I couldn't imagine life without him. The support and wisdom he offered all of us in the family was invaluable. At the age of 62 he was diagnosed with a very rare form of cancer that is induced by a chemical exposure and only 1% of cancer victims survive it. We watched him progress in four months, from the tennis courts, to gone by March 6th. The impact on me was profound, as he had been my mentor and inspiration.

After my father died I began to see substantial changes taking place in my husband who was now 45; changes in attitude towards his responsibilities as a father and husband. Within a year's time he was asking for a divorce and the battle was on to save my marriage. He seemed to feel time was running out for him and he needed to live life to the fullest while he could. Two years down the road, in the midst of all this anxiety, I woke up one morning with a purple mass on my own chest. It was in three good-sized raised patches. I remembered the doctors saying when they performed surgery on my father two years prior that there were patches of purple mass on the outside lining of his bladder.

I called my gynecologist and he took me right in that morning. He took one look at me and said, "Judy I'm sending you over now to the Breast Cancer Center in New Hampshire. I'll make the appointment." By 5:30 that very afternoon they had diagnosed me with the exact same type of cancer my father had died of two years earlier. This was a Friday afternoon and I remember walking to my car thinking, I must have been exposed to the same chemical as well.

A strong impression began to form in my mind. I felt that I was being given a choice to choose life or to go with this. I actually contemplated both options, which surprised me, and I realized I must be suffering from some depression that I wasn't aware of. I thought of my three sons and immediately I felt the responsibility for them and their young lives and I cried out to God to save me for their sakes. I was scheduled for surgery the following Tuesday.

When I moved to Dublin, New Hampshire, I had joined a wonderful local nondenominational church where the pastor had been doing some teaching on healing. The elders had been laying hands on people and praying for them and healings were taking place. I thought about calling them and seeking prayer, but then due to the location of the mass I thought better of it and decided I had better pray for this myself. I crawled into bed that evening and before going to sleep I laid my hand on the mass crying out to my Heavily Father, my great physician, to come and heal me, in Jesus name.

The next morning when I awoke I was surprised to see the mass had all turned brown. This was Saturday morning. Then Sunday morning when I awoke, the mass was gone, leaving behind pink skin where it had been. Monday morning upon waking, the pink skin had turned to light brown and by Tuesday morning there was no sign of the cancerous mass at all, IT WAS GONE!

My Heavenly Father and my great physician had sent his angels to "TOUCH" me and make me whole again.

I went in for my appointment and the doctor stood in amazement. He had no words! Regaining his composure, he asked, what did you do? I had done nothing but pray, bringing it before my Heavenly Father in the name of His Son.

I learned something brand-new about our wonderful God that day. That we serve a Heavenly Father who is longing for us to bring our concerns to Him first allowing Him to "TOUCH" us with his wonderful hand of healing. Prior to this experience, I had always gone to man for my solutions and when all else failed, then I tried God. Now I knew the reverse was true and I began to bring all matters before Him first, allowing Him to rule and reign in my life through the power of His "LOVE."

Our heavenly father is waiting to enter your heart. Won't you open the door of your heart and invite him to come in, bringing His healing Love into your life today?

Psalms 34:7-8

The angel of the Lord encamps around those who fear him, and he delivers them. Taste and see that the Lord is good; blessed is the one who takes refuge in him. (NIV)

Chapter 17

Notified

Summertime had finally arrived and the fast-paced school year had come to a close. The college kids on campus had headed for home and once again the village was ours. A quiet peace had settled in on our mountaintop. My son Todd, who was attending the local liberal arts college at the time, was about to arrive home for lunch from his summer job. There was a warm breeze blowing so I decided to prepare food for us to eat on the deck where we could relax and enjoy the view of the valley below.

As Todd and I were experiencing the true essence of summer and the conversation of the day, I began to feel an uneasiness, almost a foreboding feeling. I quickly brushed it aside as I so much wanted to enjoy the day. But then it came again, this time with more force than before. Like it or not, I had to acknowledge it. What was it? Something was very, very wrong.

Turning to Todd, I began to share what I was feeling. He said, "you know mom, I've been feeling something like that myself for the last few minutes." We both bowed our heads right there in that place seeking the Lord as to how to pray. Strong impressions came right away that my son Eric was in grave danger and that we needed to pray for angels to protect and intervene.

A few months earlier at Christmas time, Eric had given his girlfriend a surprise gift trip to Hawaii. The date had finally arrived and they were off experiencing the sheer tropical beauty of Kauai. One of their dreams was to hike up a mountain trail that led to a beautiful natural waterfall that fell into an emerald pool below.

This was that day. They left early in the morning along with a few others and arriving by noon they were thrilled to see the beauty of the place and experience the wonders of nature. There was no hint of the pending danger around the corner. Early in the afternoon the clouds suddenly began to gather and the rain began to pour. Eric decided they had better head back as they were several hours from their car. As they began their descent, rivers of water began to flow past them on both sides of the trail. These rivers seemed to be gaining in size, and they quickly realized they were in a flash flood!

Being young, they stepped up their speed, but the force of the storm was still gaining on them. The water on both sides of the trail was beginning to converge to form one power-ful cascade of water down this mountainside. Coming upon a rise in the trail an island was beginning to form. Eric surveyed the situation and decided that he would cut a small tree down with the knife he happened to have on him and ride the log down the river to get some help. He suggested that the five of them remain on this raised island as he moved ahead with his plan.

Eric proceeded to cut and trim the tree, then zipping his knife into his pants pocket, he entered the water. It was rougher than he thought.

There was a lot of debris and boulders to deal with everywhere. Everything was moving fast and going dangerously out of control. Suddenly, his log caught boulders on both sides of the river, throwing him under the log feet first. He managed to catch a grip on the log with both hands and hang on but the force of the water was greater than his own strength. He needed to pull himself up under the log and then work his way onto the top of the log. Only then might he have a chance to work his way to one side or the other, escaping the overpowering force of the river. But try as he might he could not find the strength to pull against the power of the water.

Meanwhile, Todd and I, not dreaming of the danger Eric was in, began to pray, crying out to God, "come and spare Eric's life, Oh Lord, whatever the circumstances. Please come and intervene!"

Eric, now at the end of his strength, decided to try one more time to pull himself up and out of danger all the while doubting in his own mind that he could do it. As he began to pull, more strength and energy began to come. He was able to pull himself up and under the log, then reaching over the top of the log with his leg he was able to right himself on top. As he assessed the situation now at hand, there just wasn't a safe exit. The distance on his left between the log and the shore was too great to reach. The distance on the right, between where he sat and a boulder that was fairly large near him, seemed to be his only option. This exit would require him to jump with arms wide open causing his chest to impact the boulder first, then his hands could cup around it, he thought, and he could pull himself up and out of the water at that point. If he could successfully make the jump he was quite sure he could propel himself from the boulder to the shore.

The attempt was successful but it bruised some of his ribs and chest, however, he was then able to hang on from there, pull himself up and out of the water and jump to shore. Now the shoreline was lined with bamboo too thick to penetrate. The sky was getting dark and the rain was still falling. He wondered about his girlfriend and the others; was there still enough island for them to rest on?

He pulled out his jackknife and begin cutting his way out. He could hear a helicopter in the distance and he wondered if they were looking for him and the others. Time seemed to be standing still and he wondered if he would ever get through this jungle of bamboo? In the early morning hours Eric broke out into freedom and he was able to reach the search and rescue crew. By telling them where to find the others, all were saved!

Eric shared this story with us when he returned home. He was surprised to hear we had been "notified" by His most powerful and loving God, to pray for him. In response, our wonderful Heavenly Father had sent his angels to empower Eric that day when he found himself in a situation beyond human strength or control. Thank you Father for extending your invisible Hand to save Eric in his hour of greatest need!

Nahum 1:7

The Lord is good, a refuge in times of trouble. He cares for those who trust in him.

Chapter *18*

Angels in the House

My husband and I had accepted a call to a prayer ministry in Washington, DC in 2005. The Sanctuary of Prayer was established in 1980 by The American Christian Trust. It was a stately home strategically positioned directly across from the Israeli Embassy. This was a spiritual retreat where some of our nation's spiritual leaders could come in and bring their team members to pray and strategize.

Many local ministries loved to come in for an afternoon or evening as well, to seek the Lord for new vision or to pray through an old one. It was truly an inspirational, spiritually rich place where you could feel the presence of the Lord in a special way. A place set apart for Him.

One afternoon in late spring a local ministry had booked a luncheon with us. I had decided to fix a California favorite, Taco Salad, and I was busy scurrying around trying to pull it all together in time. The living room in this antique home had been beautifully appointed with registered furniture, some from the Lincoln estate and some from George Washington's estate. The fabric used to upholster the couch and two chairs in the living room had been donated by First Lady Nancy Reagan. It was a beautiful brocade with raspberry pink and cream stripes. A one-of-a-kind fabric to say the least.

For this particular luncheon, I chose to serve it as a buffet from the dining room to accommodate the large crowd of people. Right on time the doorbell began to ring and they streamed in prepared for a lovely afternoon. As the ladies were serving themselves and chatting, suddenly a woman rushed in from the living room to announce that her plate had slipped from her hand, turned upside down and had landed in the center of a cushion on the couch! She had tried to pick it up and clean it but when I rushed out to take a look there was a 12-inch circular oil spot on the cushion, and oil had splashed up on the side pillows as well.

I don't normally put so much importance on material items but this truly was a special fabric, on a special couch, in a special place and I was just a little bit worried as to how the owner was going to receive this news. I brushed it off and said, "don't worry about it, I'll just put a paper towel over it for now and take care of it later."

By the time my husband and I were finished with our ministry that day it was midnight, and we were tired so I decided to take the two small pillows, place them in the downstairs laundry room and call it a day.

The next morning, venturing upstairs and into the living room, I was in for the shock of my life. The cushion was perfect, there were no signs of the oil stain or salsa - nothing! There was literally no evidence that anything had ever been spilled on that cushion. I knew angels had been in the house. They had miraculously cleaned the cushion removing every trace of salsa and the oil.

I had a hard time at first believing this magnificent, wonderful God I serve would care so much about something so seemingly insignificant, from a heavenly perspective. I just stood there for a few minutes in utter amazement. I had not even prayed about it or asked him for help, and yet he just showed up, sending His angels to save the day.

Then I remembered the two cushions downstairs in the laundry room and thought, oh no, I should have left them on the couch. We went racing down the stairs and into that laundry room only to discover that angels had visited there too and the pillows were both in perfect condition.

Who is this God who "intimately" knows and cares for us, who created the heavens and the earth and all the people on it? Could it be that he is a God who knows when we rise and when we lie down, when we come in and when we go out? A God who has explored our hearts and knows our every care.

Oh God, It is the most amazing feeling to know how deeply you care about us inside and out, and the realization of it is so great, that I cannot comprehend it!

Joel 2:27-29

Return to me and you will know that I live among my people Israel and that I, the Eternal One, am your God and there is no other. Never again will My people be shamed among the nations. Then in those days I will pour out My Spirit to all humanity; your children will boldly and prophetically speak the word of God. Your elders will dream dreams; your young warriors will see visions. No one will be left out. (The Voice)

Chapter *19*

Insomnia's Cure

The new year was rolling in with a dramatic start. I was feeling the need to have a few days of rest after many dinners, shopping, and overnight guests from the holiday season, when one morning the phone rang unexpectedly at 2:00 am. I thought wow, who calls at 2:00 am?

Reaching over for my phone, I said hello, with a bit of trepidation. On the other end of the line I heard the voice of an old friend who was now a pastor in South Korea. She apologized for the ungodly hour and asked me if I might be willing to pray for her friend Kim, as he had not been able to sleep for seven days.

Kim was on a special assignment for the government of South Korea and tensions were running high. President Parks had loaned her Buddhist priest to minister to Kim, but to no avail.

I sent up a quick prayer for guidance, and said of course I'd be happy to pray with him. As Kim took the phone and began to speak to me, I was immediately touch by his gracious desire to not impose his problems on me. This was truly a caring and sensitive human being, I thought, and I proceeded to ask him if he might like to try Jesus who was the prince of peace and sleep.

He said "Okay, why not?" I proceeded to lead him in a prayer, asking Jesus to come into his heart that night, and to break the cycle of insomnia, declaring that the power of God's love and peace trumped all.

The next morning Kim gave me a call and he said "I fell into a deep sleep for 12 hours and during that time, I had a dream of Jesus who invited me to come and walk with him. He said he loved me and that He had a wonderful plan for my life, should I choose to seek Him for it."

Kim seemed genuinely amazed, and he asked me if I would be willing to pray with him once a week. So the date was set, and we started on a journey together of discovering all that the Lord had for Him.

As time unfolded, I began to feel the Lord prodding me to send him a Life Application NIV Bible, where he could read the word and be guided by the commentary below, personalizing the text for him. I purchased the Bible and got his address from my friend and shipped it off. In about 10 days I received a call from Kim and he said, "I came home from work tonight to find a package at my gate, I couldn't believe it sat there all day long without being stolen. The address on the package was addressed to the other side of the city of Seoul and I don't understand how it was delivered here." Then he said, "it must be Jesus who brought this Bible to me! I will be sure and read it. Where should I begin?"

I directed him to the Book of John, and his heart began to soar with love for his new found Savior and Friend. He felt so passionately about the Lord that he started a series of oil paintings depicting different aspects of Jesus and his teachings. He completed eight in all. Painting became a creative form of worship for Kim and the Lord's presence greatly blessed him in this new place of discovery.

Kim saw his "Bible arrival" as a large miracle, but I saw the heart of a man forever changed and I don't know about you, but I believe that was the greatest miracle of all.

Psalms 28:6-7

Praise be to the Lord, for he has heard my cry for mercy. The Lord is my strength and my shield; my heart trusts in him, and he helps me. My heart leaps for joy, and with my song I praise him. (NIV)

Chapter 20

A Thief Held Captive

It was 1995 in the picturesque valley of Napa, California where grape vines climb up the hillsides and new wine flows in the fall. I owned a full service salon in the quaint village of St. Helena. The Lord had been filling my chair with people who were hungry to know him, and the 1886 stone chapel next door was filling fast.

On this particular day I was on my way to Southern California where a ministry was hosting a special conference on prayer. In preparing to leave town I needed to stop by the salon and drop off some supplies and then continue on to the San Francisco airport. In a rush, I pulled up behind the salon with my windows down, leaving my wallet sitting on the passenger seat.

Entering the salon, the girls seemed to be full of questions that day, and by the time I was exiting twenty minutes had passed by. I felt I was still okay as it was an hour and a half to reach the airport which still left an hour and a half for check-in. When I opened the door of my car I noticed my wallet was not on the passenger seat. I looked everywhere, but to no avail.

A sick feeling began to creep into my stomach and I knew I had blown it. By moving too fast, leaving my window open, door unlocked, I had left a wallet on the seat in full view. I was so unhappy with myself. I thought it was clearly my careless mistake, and I sure as heck can't ask the Lord to rescue me now. So I said, "well, Lord, I'm so sorry, but I've brought this on myself in my rushing around, and if you want me to fly today, somehow you will have to get me on the plane without my ID."

What I didn't know was this was the weekend of the Unabomber scare at the San Francisco airport and now security was not only asking for one picture ID, but two. I was running a bit late so I stepped on it and arrived there in record time. When I entered the United check-in to secure my ticket, I noticed the lines were unusually long, and moving very slowly. It wasn't until I was about third in line that I began to overhear the conversation at the counter between the attendant and a 15-year old boy. They were asking him for two picture ID's and he didn't have a driver's license yet, then they proceeded to tell him he could not fly until his father made some other arrangements. His father was in Seattle, Washington, and that was his destination. I thought wow, how am I ever going to pass security and get on that plane!

When I approached the attendant I said, "I know this sounds hard to believe but I had my wallet stolen off the seat of my car two hours ago and I have no ID." She looked at me long and hard and then said, "I know what we'll do with you," as she took my suitcase and carry-on, sending me on to a special examination area. Suddenly, swinging from behind me and in my face, were two Fox News reporters, with a very large camera. They proceeded to ask me, "Ma'am, how does it feel to be a Unabomber suspect?" I was shocked. I hadn't heard anyone talking about it so this was my first time hearing about the "fear" of the day at the San Francisco airport. So I said with great surprise, "What?" and they repeated their question. Then I said, "well, I guess with the X-rays of myself and my luggage it should be a safe trip."

I was right, for after X-raying me and my luggage they found nothing and concluded, with a prearranged ticket, there was no good reason why I couldn't fly. So on the plane I went, laughing to myself over the clearance the Lord had arranged. I must say the song Amazing Grace took on a whole new meaning that day.

The conference was scheduled to run Tuesday through Thursday and it was a packed house. Hundreds of people had arrived from all over California. The leadership had heard about my lost wallet and the Lord's divine intervention so they asked me if I'd be willing to share. I said I'd be happy to, thinking the story was over, not realizing the Lord had   another surprise in store for me. When I awoke Thursday morning, the last day of the conference, I was feeling the loss of my wallet and all that it contained, including $227 in cash. I thought wow, Lord, I really need my wallet, and just because I foolishly left my window open, door unlocked, and wallet in plain sight, it still does not condone theft. So Lord, I am praying a guilt trip on the person who stole it and I'm asking you to impress them to return it intact.

During the 10:30 coffee break that morning I decided to check my phone messages. Sure enough there were calls to return. One of the calls was from the Vasconi Drug Store in town which I found puzzling as I didn't use their pharmacy, as one of my clients owned the other pharmacy in town. I proceeded to call and reached the lady at the front desk, who said, "we just wanted you to know someone has mysteriously left your wallet on our counter. We didn't see who it was but everything seems to be here including $227 in cash."

Tears began to well up in my eyes and I said, "it has been four days since it was stolen. I can't believe they returned it this late, with everything still in it, including $227 cash." We paused in awe over the grace and loving care of our most wonderful, personal, every ready to forgive and restore Heavenly Father. Oh, what a God of mercy and grace we serve.

Psalms 31:1-4

In you, Lord, I have taken refuge; let me never be put to shame; deliver me in your righteousness. Turn your ear to me, come quickly to my rescue; be my rock of refuge, a strong fortress to save me. Since you are my rock and my fortress, for the sake of your name lead and guide me. Keep me free from the trap that is set for me, for you are my refuge. (NIV)

Chapter *21*

Frozen Transmission

This particular year had been especially demanding on my car as I was traveling to various locations in northern California for meetings and conferences. I decided it was time to shop for a new one. Opening the paper one morning I saw a full page ad by Nissan. They were offering a 1-1/2 % loan package for those with good credit scores. So I decided to clear my schedule and head over the mountain to the Nissan dealership and see what they might have on their lot. Of course as you might have guessed, a few hours later I was driving a beautiful new Maxima home. As I pulled into the garage all seemed well and I was excited.

The next morning I needed to drive into the Bay Area for a meeting and I was feeling relieved that I would be driving a new car as the location of this meeting was not in the safest neighborhood and this town had a record for high crime.

Grabbing my purse and briefcase, I climbed into the car and was on my way. Everything seemed to be perfectly in order. Storm clouds were gathering but no rain had fallen yet; traffic was light, allowing me to arrive right on time. Much to my surprise I found a parking place in a schoolyard where families and faculty were coming and going and it felt safe and comfortable.

My meeting came to a close around 5:30 pm and as I walked back out into the school parking lot I noticed that everyone was gone and my car was now standing alone. I immediately had an uneasy feeling as the sun was setting and I felt a great urgency to head home. Climbing into the car I turned on the ignition and, resting my hand on the center console shift, I tried to pull it out of park. It was frozen in its place and would not budge! I tried it again, and once more it would not move. After playing around with it for 15 minutes or so I decided I had better call the auto club and see what they might be able to do.

About 30 minutes later a large middle aged man showed up from AAA and it was now dark. I was feeling a bit uncomfortable as we were now the only two people left in this parking lot. Climbing into the driver's seat the mechanic began to examine the problem. He experimented with this and with that but nothing would move the frozen handle out of park.

After an hour he looked at me and said, "Ma'am, I'm afraid I can't help you out." I looked at him and said, "well when all else fails let's try Jesus." I proceeded to pray, asking the Lord to come and heal my car. Then resting his hand on the shifter he proceeded to pull it out of park and into place. We both looked at each other in complete amazement. Shrugging my shoulders, I said, "I guess God even cares about frozen transmissions." As he was getting out of the car he turned to me and said, "ma'am, it might be wise for you to head right home now," and that's just what I did.

After an hour and a half I was safely parked in my garage, thanking God profusely for rescuing me. But all was not well with this new automobile, for the very next morning when I tried to leave for work the shifter once again was frozen in park. This time I tried Jesus first and once again I was able to pull the handle into gear and back out of my garage.

I knew then that I needed to head right back to the Nissan dealership and let them examine this new car. Arriving safely now at their auto repair division, I explained what had happened the evening before. After the mechanics examined the handle they said, ma'am the parts holding the shifter in place are simply missing. It is impossible for this shifter to have moved into place and stayed there. I don't see how you were able to drive the car at all. I told them the story of what happened and we all stood there amazed as they had seen me drive the car into the parking lot.

Who would have thought that our wonderful God, creator of the heavens and the earth would

125

care about a frozen transmission? As I headed back home that day, I turned to the Lord and said, "I had no idea Lord that you are so present in my life knowing when I go out and when I come in, when I lie down and when I rise." I knew then that angels are still about their Heavenly Father's business, miraculously intervening for His Kids as they call out to Him in their times of trouble.

Psalms 30:1

I will exalt you, Lord, for you lifted me out of the depths and did not let my enemies gloat over me. Lord my God, I called to you for help, and you healed me. You, Lord, brought me up from the realm of the dead; you spared me from going down to the pit. (NIV)

Chapter 22

A Miracle Interrupts
the Sunday Sermon

There is a cultural attitude that prevails in many minds today that says, when the going gets tough, a mind-altering drug is the solution. They reach out to self-medicating to escape their pain. I would like to share a story with you that portrays the amazing love of God and His solution.

I was serving as a pastor in Lake County, California. My assignment was to establish new prayer ministries in some of the local churches. Diana Blackburn, a pastor of the Middletown Community Church, had invited me to attend a Sunday service to assess some of the current needs there.

A powerful drug culture had worked its way into the whole county and was robbing the best from those who were drawn into it. The responsible adults and pastoral leadership were greatly concerned. A myriad of teens and young adults were caught up in this deceptive mindset that was dangerously carrying them off in a whirlwind and dropping them at death's door.

I arrived a bit early this Sunday to allow some time for connecting with people I was currently mentoring. The pastor and I had become good friends and I was excited about what I felt the Lord had for all of us that morning. The music began to play, encouraging each of us to take our seats. Everything seemed quite normal.

After a few announcements were made, a visiting speaker stood and walked to the podium. About halfway through his sermon he suddenly stopped with his eyes gazing into the center of row eight and asked, "Jimmy are you all right?"

Jimmy, with his dusty blond hair and bright blue eyes, had been one of those who was caught up in addiction, and about eight months earlier he had suffered a major heart attack. The pastor had been ministering to him whereby he had repented, choosing to leave the world of addiction and depend on Jesus. The Lord had touched him with a healing touch and he had been experiencing good health and freedom from years of addiction.

The eyes of the whole congregation turned now and focused on Jimmy, wondering what went wrong? Jimmy was on the floor writhing in great pain with his shoulders turned towards each other and his chest caving inward, gasping for air. As a visitor, I paused and waited for the leadership to make a move, but no one did. Everyone seemed paralyzed by the scene. Then the Lord spoke to me and said, "go pray for Jimmy now or he will die."

I stood up and while moving into the aisle towards Jimmy I began to cry out to the Lord for direction. My spiritual eyes were opened and I saw a dark form about 9 feet tall standing on the left side of Jimmy. I felt impressed that it was the angel of death who was there ready to take him. I rebuked this angel in Jesus name and commanded him to leave now! I saw him literally leave like a vapor and he was gone.

I felt impressed that Jimmy was using again, turning to a drug rather than Jesus and that it was idolatrous in the sight of God. I knew it was eclipsing the Lord's ability to intervene as he so desired to do at this moment. I asked Jimmy if he was using and he said, "yes, pot." I asked him if he wanted to repent and he said yes and that he did in front of the whole congregation. I felt to declare life over him and that he would live now in Jesus name that he would finish the course the Lord had set before him when he had placed Jimmy in his mother's womb. That the God of all mercy and grace was giving Jimmy a second chance to be redeemed.

The heart attack stopped immediately and he began to straighten up, taking some deep breaths. The congregation all breathed sighs of relief as well and the pastor resumed his preaching. After the service was over the Lord spoke to me again and said, "I want you to find Jimmy and ask him if he would be willing to set up a weekly mentoring appointment with you for a while."

For the next year and a half Jimmy came weekly for his appointment and I had a front row seat, watching our wonderful God heal and deliver this young man from the culture of drugs and death. He landed a special job at St. Helena Hospital and Health Center where he walked out his new healthy lifestyle, receiving the blessings of being a positive healthy contributor not only to his own life but to the life of his community. This was a wonderful, miraculous transformation for all to see, out of the clutches of death into the hands of a most merciful, life giving God.

MY PRAYER:

Oh, Lord, may your love, as demonstrated through signs, wonders and miracles break through our difficulties and propel us into our destiny. When we reach up to you for our breakthrough, we will be counting on your invisible hand to move, bringing the change that truly alters for the good, the outcome of our impossible circumstances!

Matthew 6:33
Seek ye first the kingdom of God, and all these things will be added unto you. (KJV)

Made in the USA
Middletown, DE
07 September 2018